A HORSE WITH HOLES IN IT

Southern Messenger Poets

Dave Smith, *Series Editor*

A HORSE WITH HOLES IN IT

POEMS

GREG ALAN BROWNDERVILLE

LOUISIANA STATE UNIVERSITY PRESS

BATON ROUGE

Published by Louisiana State University Press
Copyright © 2016 by Greg Alan Brownderville
All rights reserved
Manufactured in the United States of America
LSU Press Paperback Original
First printing

Designer: Laura Roubique Gleason
Typeface: Minion Pro
Printer and binder: LSI

Library of Congress Cataloging-in-Publication Data

Names: Brownderville, Greg Alan, author.
Title: A horse with holes in it : poems / Greg Alan Brownderville.
Description: Baton Rouge : Louisiana State University Press, [2016]
Identifiers: LCCN 2016005887| ISBN 978-0-8071-6354-2 (pbk. : alk.
  paper) | ISBN 978-0-8071-6355-9 (pdf) | ISBN 978-0-8071-6356-6 (epub)
  | ISBN 978-0-8071-6357-3 (mobi)
Classification: LCC PS3602.R728 A6 2016 | DDC 811/.6—CIPdc23
LC record available at http://lccn.loc.gov/2016005887

To my brother, Eric Brownderville, who taught me to go by feel

Verily the dawn is the head . . . , the sun its eye, the wind its breath, the mouth the Vaisvanara fire, the year the body of the sacrificial horse. Heaven is the back, the sky the belly, the earth the chest, the quarters the two sides, the intermediate quarters the ribs, the members the seasons, the joints the months and half-months, the feet days and nights, the bones the stars, the flesh the clouds. The half-digested food is the sand, the rivers the bowels, the liver and the lungs the mountains, the hairs the herbs and trees. As the sun rises, it is the forepart; as it sets, the hindpart . . . When the horse shakes itself, then it lightens. When it kicks, it thunders. When it makes water, it rains. Voice is its voice.

—from the *Brihadaranyaka Upanishad* (translated by Max Müller)

This can be illustrated by the output of a handful of individuals who have developed protolanguage beyond what are, today at least, its normal limits. These are the inventors of makeshift, idiosyncratic languages: children, almost always twins, who for one reason or another are more than usually involved with each other . . .

da   kjob   hoto   krei   loch   ich   du   mach
there snow   horse   more   hole   I   you   make
'Over there in the snow you and I made a horse with holes in it'

—from *Language and Species*, by Derek Bickerton

CONTENTS

ACKNOWLEDGMENTS

I thank the editors of the following publications for printing versions of the poems indicated.

Arcadia: "Prosimetrum 1: Assorted Heads"; *Arkansas Review:* "Welcome to the Old Cathedral"; *Blackbird:* "Prosimetrum 3: The Homemade Fireworks"; *The Boiler:* "Easy," "A Message for the King," and "Prosimetrum 2: Body Shots"; *Five Points:* "Honest Gospel Singing"; *Hick Poetics* (anthology): "After a Sunday Morning Visit," "Song for a Kiss," and "Walkin' in Memphis"; *Iron Horse Literary Review:* "Walkin' in Memphis," "Neither Fire nor the Death of Fire," and "Sweet Tooth Homeless"; *Poetry Daily:* "After a Sunday Morning Visit"; *Rumba Under Fire* (anthology): "Theater in Wartime"; *Southwest Review:* "After a Sunday Morning Visit"; *Virginia Quarterly Review:* "Song for a Kiss."

Special thanks to Dave Smith for giving me a place among the Southern Messenger Poets; to the Sewanee Writers' Conference for supporting me with a Walter E. Dakin Fellowship; to Hendrix College for making me a 2013 Hendrix-Murphy Visiting Writer; to my friends at SMU for being so extraordinarily kind to me; to Hicks Wogan for saying I had to write "Song for a Kiss"; to my students, past and present, for adding much joy and meaning to my life; to Chad White for reading this entire book in manuscript and giving me encouragement and sound advice; to Tim Cassedy for finding the missing magical puzzle piece; to Tarfia Faizullah for "Hey, Greg" and bourbon; to Sebastián Páramo, Charles Wuest, Dan Moss, and Johnny Wink for valuable advice on several of these poems; to sweet Amelia and the Dickens for all the campfire times; to Eli Burrell for a notion not to break; to Brooks Lee, Babbie Lovett, and Rod Kidwell for their Jaguar spirit; to Pamela Jane Brownderville for making sure I found that perfect crayon, the color of the primer palomino; to core members of The Mirror Saw for accepting me when I was a child, letting me enter the Temple of the Twins, and teaching me songs and spells that charge my poems to this day; and to Alton Brownderville for telling me a dark and vivid story about a horse with holes in it.

A HORSE WITH HOLES IN IT

HONEST GOSPEL SINGING

When I was a kid, I went to church.
I sang in church: from the time I was twelve,
I did a special every Sunday.
And often, when the preacher preached, I nodded yes
like a boat motor bobbing
down the highway toward the lake.

My fancier companions took me to the lake
in high school and college. I remember
floating tipsy, grazing bridges with fingertips.
I remember picnics on the party barge
and being a helpful kid, twisting lids
off jars for women. I remember
some of my life.

But last night, home
for the first time in a long time,
when I walked into my dark boyhood bedroom,
I was slapping blind: my hand
didn't know where the light switch was anymore.

And this morning in church,
when the preacher asked me to sing, I rose quietly
and walked to the front—slow,
like a spooky old man through a kindergarten classroom,
there to learn with the other children
how to sound things out.
And though I started all right, the second verse
wouldn't come home to me. I muttered
melodically. Nonsense syllables.

But the people broke out in tongues—
they wept, and said some mystery words
like *shahn-die*, seconding my gibberish with God's,
because they know. They know
honest gospel singing when they hear it.

NEITHER FIRE NOR THE DEATH OF FIRE

As we were toggling down the street one morning,
the sun's flashing face
cracked my skull, and I looked up
at the ghostlike Capitol ahead.
"Giant spark plug?" I mumbled.

Jill squinted,
said, "I can't think about that right now."

Dress shoes walked their people to church,
stepping over Saturday night's
colorful smithereens.
At our feet a zillion ants
transformed a discarded, half-eaten sandwich
into a paradox: motion and
stillness.

Jill squinted up at the Capitol.
"Giant fire hydrant?" she mumbled.

"Here we are," I said.
"Hard, gemlike flames."

The sun pulled the covers over its face.

Stumbling up from the park,
a lone soldier, drunk
in her pixilated camo, fondled the left breast
of a parking meter. Jill glanced at me,
her gray irises and small pupils
like unsharpened pencil ends.
Something
was all but happening.
We were all
but lovers, the world
all but real.

THEATER IN WARTIME

For the play we got ourselves in love. Otherwise
        I didn't know her.
There were no other players. For three weeks
        of rehearsals, we lived together,
going by our characters' names, smelling like each other.
        The city turned into a war. Explosions
            gashed sky
      day and night, left both of us
          sick to the marrow.

The day of the first performance, the bombs
          louder, closer,
      we made love again and again.
When the hour came, like a demented mailman, the city
           made no sound. We stepped out
        into the smoking ruins and held each other.
Then trusted our feet, soles clicking
        toward the playhouse. I hoped
                it still existed.

      No one else there, doors bolted shut.
I took a dead potted plant from the street and flung it
        through a ground-floor window, kicked out
the jagged fangs of glass, and climbed in.
        I doubted
she would follow, but she did.

      We busied ourselves with exercises, the normal routines.
    Got dressed, patted on our makeup.
Then readied the equipment as best we could, adjusting
        the lights to an all-purpose setting.

And strode onstage. *So soon?*

We looked into each other. The void
gnawed away
                     at my peripheral vision. *Now,*
      I thought. *The crew, the crowd—*
they'll all appear, and the apocalypse
        unhappen.
               Now.

    The first line
was mine.
         Simple. *Say the line.*

I couldn't. I could not
   speak words. She waited
for a moment,
            a few moments,
      then stepped back.
Her face darkened and wilted
      like a page cast into a fire.

CAENEUS AND THE BASKET BEARER

Even when they graced the Parthenon,
starring in frieze and metope, the finest
comic strips the world has ever known,
they grieved. Lapith and basket bearer, though dressed
in toy-bright coats of paint, were never blessed
to live soul-free like plastic superheroes.
They sensed each other through the wall—so close,

born and sworn to their twin dimensions, blocked
by pride and fear. She was the magic key
to his soft core sealed in Pentelic rock.
He craved her even as she hurt to be
with him. In the fifth century BC,
Phidias rendered them in their unblemished
pageantry: wondrous work he thought he finished

but scarce began. The oldest sculptor, death's
dependable accomplice, ravaged it,
crumbling the virgin's icy visage and the youth's
fixed feet. As though the staged, balletic bout
with centaurs raged and wrecked the world, time cut
our stubborn lovers down and weathered all
their sinews to the color of pure soul.

Two sufferers—a woman, a queer brute—
stand naked in their need. Fractured from wrought
perfections, paneled myths that distanced them,
only for one another they are broken
beautiful—if they touched, they would be home.
But she is guarded in a French museum,
and he a captive alien in London.

HOW HE KNOWS

The singer is up late—humming and strumming
in his dark studio. Across the room,
the pocket of his bright-blue poplin jacket
goes luminescent. He puts his guitar down,
fetches the phone. She's texting him again:
"Go look outside. There's a me-moon in the sky.
My face, I swear."
                              He texts back, "Would it look
the same up here?"
                              She replies, "There's only
one moon we human beings have to look at."

Four years, long years, since the last time they touched.
The singer hides, nine states away, in Maine.
The other night he called her. "Lately," she said,
"I've been putting you on speakerphone
so my baby girl will learn your voice.
I can't believe she's turning two next month."

As he hugs his Martin, plucks it whisper-tipped,
his humming suddenly has moonlight in it.
Freak bout of nineteenth-century emotion.
He forces half a laugh. Lovers' moons,
he knows, are mints and mothballs. Did they become
fraudulent first in life or in song? Whichever.
The music swelling in him, thank the dead lord,
will never be inflicted on the world.

No one is watching as he grabs his jacket
and staggers into the chill night. He thinks
about the little girl, a stranger getting
to know him as a voice. All he is
to anyone. He zips his jacket up.
Translucent clouds are moving like calm surf.
In the distance: hills clichéd with snow, a sky

clichéd with stars. He walks backward, then forward,
side to side, as if drunk or dazed—a man
desperately searching heaven for a moon.
There is no moon. Heaven is a museum.
The twee old wishing stars have gone extinct
and, nights like this, are only simulated
to show what love was like. That's how he knows
they aren't alive and bioluminescent,
swimming with his wet, astonished eyes.

AFTER A SUNDAY MORNING VISIT

My grandmother—"Two-Mama"—lived right there,
a clothesline from my parents.
I remember Ts of cedar,
taut wire, and swatting laundry. In trucks and cars,
many thousands
of times, I've backed out awkwardly to miss
the posts—I guess I've even done it since
she died and they were plucked from the earth, done it by force
of habit until
today, when suddenly it's ritual,
suddenly it's this.

As mosquito hawks hover above my car,
Two-Mama and her son,
my Uncle Vance, appear
in the drive, ghosts or tricks of memory.
A simple scene:
their easy grins, those rugged posts that stood
for half a century on this mangy lawn.
I remember "coke-top shooters": crude weapons me
and Uncle Vance
made out of clothespins, boards, and rubber bands.
Mine was painted red.

When mosquito hawks lit on the line, we'd launch
our mini flying saucers,
magical logos, and watch
them zoom toward our prey—Vance right beside me
like we were brothers,
like he was still a child and spring could last.
To him the clothesline must have seemed both curse
and blessing. I was grown before Two-Mama told me
that as a kid
he'd back up to a cedar post's dark wood
and play like he was Christ.

That was before he "lost God and stopped singing."
The crucifix came true
as I dreamed his boy-hands hanging.
Back then, she said, he had "good gospel lungs,
and sang so you
could feel his soul and feel that Latter Rain."
His fear about *no sin shall enter into*
heaven woke a wailing lonesome in his songs.
Listening, I tried
to dream his voice to life and make it light
up like a tavern's neon.

She said he dunked "old Blue" in a washtub over
and over: *I baptize you*
in the name of God the Father,
Son, and Holy Ghost till the dog drowned.
He buried Blue
in soft dirt beneath the glowing plums:
dirt that kept arrowheads like secrets, and knew
the way from Coley's ribbon-cane down to Gum Pond.
Vance was eight.
He crushed a dog's neck and felt the fight go out
again and again in dreams.

At eight I ran nose-first through sun-fresh linen.
A blur of boy so new,
in the bright of the day, I ran.
The wind was time, and time the matador
who never drew,
for all was one bright present. Nothing cost.
When my uncle died, it was me strangling Blue
in nightmares, Vance a disembodied voice in my ear:
I crossed the Cross.
Going home to hell at thirty-three because
I blasphemed Jesus Christ.

In a recurring dream, I see him walk
up to a giant tree.
I smile and say, *This oak*
gives the best shade. Like an air-conditioned room.
But he can't see
or hear me as he lies down in the cool
green light and whistles "Heaven's Jubilee."
His shirtless chest dries out and turns to soft white loam.
When I kneel
beside him, his red beard becomes an anthill,
ants coming to a boil.

I took the clothesline down three years ago
but spared a wooden T,
spared it even though
it blocked the drive and looked like it was going
back to tree:
lichens and birds' nests. It survived on sun,
arms wide to the weather—survived patiently,
until I dug it out and burned it one still morning
late last year.
Didn't want to, but I couldn't bear
to see it fall on its own.

I throw my arm around the passenger seat
like we're buds, look behind me,
cut the angle just right.
When dearest facts no longer live in muscle
memory,
this is what's left: the forcing it, relearning,
returning. Soon, I reckon, I won't see
the ghosts and the ghosts won't see me—we'll end this trouble.
But soon's not here.
Rough cedar cross, decrepit welcomer:
I'm missing you this morning.

PROSIMETRUM 1: ASSORTED HEADS

1

All the colors of the universe, wondrous clutter everywhere. Sister Law had conjured that rickety sanctum out of scrap lumber from her dead husband's building business. Called it "The Upper Room." You had to spider up a red-rung ladder to achieve the holy of holies. First time I entered, she made me climb first, gripping her bag of "leavings" and art supplies, and she was right behind me. Me and Sister Law in her highest outbuilding—a cross between a chapel and a toy shop, crazed with her sculptures. The room was her mind, and there we sat, two kids in the floor. She was eighty-five years old.

We prayed, we sang. She began to rig a boy up out of trash. She was a Oneness preacher. When I quoted Revelation, "Strengthen the things which remain," all of a country sudden, the Holy Ghost possessed us. We spoke in other tongues. Just me and Ethel Leona Fitch Law. She was sitting there making a boy.

2

Sister Law said the Father, Son, and Spirit are three of many masks. My Sunday School teacher said no. One day, he took me out walking down a rock road, along a weedy bank. Small, unseen animals moving in the brush. He said the Trinity is like that. The brush itself is alive, but certain animals are in there, snapping twigs and rustling grass.

Me and Sister Law—we sang, we prayed, we spoke in tongues. She was Oneness. She was buds with heathens. She made spooky dolls that, little did I know, would later scare my niece and nephew. Keep them from wanting to sleep in Uncle Greg's room. To me, the dolls were like speaking in tongues. To me, when you close your eyes, speaking in tongues looks like that scary snow dust in the hills, how it snake-swirls over pavement in your headlights. Unlike my niece and nephew, even at their age, I liked to be that kind of scared.

One time, me and Sister Law went to the turtle boil. Out at the hush harbor. People handled snakes and got possessed there, same as church but different. Mister Good Day used my body as a horse for better than three hours. Danced up on the women and even on the men.

Sometimes me and Sister Law would laugh in the Spirit—that was called the holy cackle. It was meant to get you good at laughing off your life.

3

She was sitting there making a boy. She painted him a shirt of picnic gingham, red and white. I think it was a boy, but the hips of the driftwood body rounded wide from a narrow waist. Sister Law painted on some blue jeans. She talked about nighttime on the inside. She said, "That outer darkness what they talk about—fact of business, it's inward. I've wandered too far in. Pure-dee old dark, son. I've been by my lonesome. Not even the Devil to torment me."

She glued on sycamore twigs for arms. Had trouble settling on a head. She had assorted orbs to choose from: a baseball smudged with green from the outfield grass, a coconut that looked like an otter's head, a real otter's head she'd taxidermied herself, a light bulb, a gourd, a shriveled apple that favored an Egyptian mummy I had seen at a museum in Memphis (Tennessee), and some I can't remember.

I had given her the baseball. My coach presented it to me after my little league game the week before because I knocked the winning home run. Sister Law liked baseball. She thought the pinch-hitter rule had ruined the American League. I wasn't sure what she was.

Light walked through the window of "The Upper Room." Sister Law held up the baseball, dirty cream, and thumbed its bruised leather. Inspected it like a vegetable she might not use for supper. She squinted at me. Made some quick strokes on the ball with a red marker. Looked at me again. Made some marks. Glued the ball atop the torso and studied on it.

She took the ball off and set the otter's head there instead. She studied on it. Tried the ball again. Tried the apple. I wondered if the glue's grip was weakening. She made marks on the coconut and gave it a chance too.

They all looked soul-worthy, all of them. In the end she settled on that hurt, grass-stained, winning smile and called the doll Yeah Boy. Sister Law was a girl.

She gave me the boy for keeps.

THE SONG—
I'm standing in the need of prayer.
Pilgrim, let me tell you—yesterday's tornado
dropped the Double Portion Tabernacle
into the Twin Oaks Mall, and made my parents' house get up
and dance.

When that ugly cloud bore down
like a black Texas, Yeah Boy quaked
on top of my dresser. His head jarred free
and rumble-rolled across my bedroom floor.

When that ugly cloud bore down, it raptured
a culvert, and they played like Slinky brothers.
A woman on the news said, "I thought
I was gonna be *blowed*
off the *globe*
of the earth."

But the wind laid down, and now I'm babbling,
I'm at large—feet bare among the burs.

There's a Ronald McDonald statue perched in a beech,
and a Stratocaster lying
in the beechdrops underneath.

A white beekeeper's suit slumbers manless
by the road, so I put it on and tromp
around and hit Mad Butcher Market.
I find a pack of matches and
a dark-chocolate bar. Matches
like pale lady hands with pink polish.
When I tap and brush them
against my candy bar, the fingertips catch fire.
They burn a yellow song
of *who am I and why*
across that small piano barcode.

My kin don't know
about my wordness, all the languages
that swarm me. They know about my Holy Ghost
possessions, but I hide the rest: how Easy
Lee and Good Day get inside
me when the Mirror Saw divides me.
Shall you compare me to a McDonald's drive-thru?
Growly guy voice
greets you, and you order a McRib. But then:
tinny girl voice (*where'd she come from?*)
offers you fries and a Coke.

I rove all over morning as The Beekeeper Spaceman. Yes,
I float across a meadow
past an abandoned game of marbles,
peer down, and dream it's our magnificent solar system.

Too hot, I shed the bee suit in the cane
and kneel like a hart beside the water brook.
A twirly-bird roof vent drifts along. I nab it,
hold it high, atop my head: a baker's hat.

I study myselves in the glassy babble.
Make a mud pie deluxe and stow it in my pocket.
Later on, I'll climb said beech
and share my pie with Ronald.

What if Ronald McDonald
is Jimi Hendrix in captivity?

Before the magical baker was, I am
a multitude. The head was never
secure. Pilgrim, please
remember. Please
remember me in prayer.

SOME WEIRD OTHER O'CLOCK

Last week I crashed my car, racing
my own thoughts
past the New Quiet Cemetery.
Jill sent a card. We're apart but
talking.

My orange '76 Pinto may never ride again.
It's at Soul Salvage, which triples
as junkyard, shouting church, and music club.
The homemade sign reads, WE MEET BY ACCIDENT.

Once, I heard a preacher say, "Jesus is
a tow truck. He will tow yo' soul on in."

Jesus has been known to leave
the beautiful dents.

· · ·

For dinner and supper, I walk
down to the corner. There's a soul-food place
with free Wi-Fi.

At the moment I'm footing it to the EASY-WAY
to purchase a personal
watermelon. Almost there.
It's morning—not yet
light outside, but will be soon. Already
the garbage truck booms apocalyptic. Noise—
there's comfort in it.
Quiet is the new loud.
It's racking when it comes, and it doesn't
come often.

· · ·

Mornings make me think of Jill.
She used to wake up in my bed,
her body lying, its position
saying 2:35 at six. She had warned me.
I remember that night
in October: She was about to fall
asleep beside me for the first time.
In 12:25 position at 12:25, she said, "I'm sorry,
but I sprawl all over the bed—I always wake up
in some weird other o'clock."

I never cared much for the gym, but mornings
we would go work out. She slogged in place
on the elliptical, her face fierce
and young, and when she pounded the treadmill,
her crowlike ponytail
pecked at the back of her head.

I have a recurring nightmare
that she dies of bird peck, Hitchcock style, and throws
herself a closed-casket funeral.
While her living version gives an embarrassed eulogy,
I sit alone in my pew
and feel guilty for not attending.

   • • •

I'm on my way back home,
passing a melodramatic furniture store.
It's been having a HUGE BLOWOUT CLEARANCE SALE
since the mid-1980s.

EVERYTHING MUST GO!

I like to imagine the morning train
from an aerial view: a magical unzipping
across the land, and when the darkness

slips off like a purple gown,
the nakedness.

I walk along
the sidewalk, personal watermelon in hand.
I see the students—hear the music, traffic, yelling.
I'm missing Jill so much, and it matters
so much. We've woken up
in some weird other o'clock.

Jill, the EASY-WAY, the BLOWOUT: they're behind me.
For now I'm with the drifters
and the grifters, the loners
and the goners, the hoopsters
and the hipsters. Loud
is the new quiet, and I'm laughing
right along, but I'll invent a better silence if
my Pinto rides again.
Reveler and reverend, I make my share of noise:
the laryngitic laughter
of an old, cold engine
mad to gun again.
I rev
because I'm desperate for the still hush
of speed.

POST-AUTHENTIC BLUES

I'm the itinerant bluesman known as
Moon Pie Robinson.

My mentor?
T-Model Ford,
genius of the party till the last
swig of Jack. Here's a Photoshopped picture.
Features me as T-Mod's trusty amanuensis.
He's telling me revisions
to his famous advice column.
As reported on Wikipedia
by me, "It was during those heady days
that Moon Pie started writing
his own soul-sopped blues about
what else
but waking up this morning."

And love. Speaking of: the punch pad
at my hometown carwash talked
with a Southern belle's breathy lilt—
"Hi thay-uh. Fuh two dollas you can
upgrade to a praymium wash."

Local gossips claim
the carwash was my high school honey.
They say I spent too many
hours there, and wouldn't date
a human. Say I used to suds up my head
and graze it with the gusher
till the lather blew clean off.

My most popular song does go:
Baby, you blow my mind.
Baby, you blow my mind.

Baby, you blow my mind,
Blow my mind like a dandelion.

Come filthy nights, the locals swear,
I long for her trigger still.

WALKIN' IN MEMPHIS

1

Woke up this morning
in Memphis, no memories to my name
of my name or how I got here.
Wandered into a boutique bar-and-gallery.
They had some metal bottle-trees
for sale. A bluesman named T-Model Ford
jangled and moaned
and talked of "Mythissippi." He said
(to his bandmates? to the crowd? to humankind?),
"T-Model Ford is
fixing to remember you sorry fuckers
how it's done."

I stepped out
and stopped below a disfigured
real tree
and asked some air named Lord to lead me home.
I didn't get an answer
other than the air, the prayer, itself.

2

I was wearing a black-and-gold sweater
I must have thrifted. Ugly as homemade sin. But.
It gave me the power of bumble flight,
so I clumsily climbed the
air. Got so high, I started laughing and couldn't stop.
The roadways down below
looked like the torso and parted thighs
of a crime-scene chalk drawing. Silver skyline,
river-mirrored,
made a key's teeth. I hovered
and buzzed above the flowery clouds.

3

Got bored, though, and eased back down to the ground.
The street was color overload. Busy
boulevard. Boulevard of lovelies. Still buzzing
a little and swigging
from my flask, I drew weird looks
from shoppers—gallants
made for magazines
and sleek-chic ladies, expensive bags
the shape of padlocks
on their arms. Got so drunk,
I felt like I was working
a Rubik's Cube with my
eyeballs.

4

I bumbled into Steak 'n Shake
for no apparent reason.
Heard a plump, overdressed man say
to another plump, overdressed man,
"It is simply a fact that a Memphis salesman
name of Robert E. Lee
does two million dollars of revenue a year
in the black hair-care industry—which,
incidentally,
is dominated by the damn Koh-reans.
Google it."

I ordered neither steak nor shake.

5

I stumbled onto Beale Street.
Some crazoes held up signs—*GOD HATES
FAGS! FAGS
DOOM
NATIONS!*

A pack of waifish twenty-somethings
came with signs of their own—
DOGS LOVE FIGS!
BATS ARE BIRDS!
I thought about the falling barns a few miles out of town.
Their doors. Unopened
envelopes from the past, or Rebel flags
just waiting for their blues and stars
and Hank Williams, Jr., grins.

6

There came a sudden madness of gray, shushing rain
as though the world had gone to static. Beale Street
was a silver river you could drown in.
I started to hallucinate. Floods, levees, fields.
Walked a wall of dirt between
the river and the rice.
Spied a face at my feet—an old sharecropper, neck deep
in Beale. I knew I knew him, but wasn't sure how.
He grinned up at me.
There were sandbags strewn about.
He used his hand to rake dirt
into a bag, then pushed it into the water and kicked
it into the levee down below.
"Plugging muskrat holes," he chirped,
"to keep the water off my rice. God honors work!"
And the water rose to his mustache, and the water
went over his head. He stood there,
rooted. Never took his eyes off mine, staring
at me from below the wavery surface
till he was good and dead. And still
he stared. I wobbled to my knees.
I felt as melty as I must have looked
to the old man's dying eyes. But then
the levee was only the sidewalk,
the river only the street, the tourists

still the tourists—and I
was drawing looks.

I feel I had a family once.
The dead man was our friend. I can't
remember.
Tiny teeth and claws come
scraping at the inside of my skull
first thing in the morning
and last thing at night.

And nobody
on this earth knows who I am.

ELEGY ON THE CREME DROP

Chocolate thimbles filled
with vanilla, right there on the kitchen table—
his mother's mother kept them around
when he was little.
Old Fashioned Creme Drops.
He loved to say
creme
drop
or only roll it
in his mind mouth. Such good words.
He didn't know. Always
there were creme drops
on his mother's mother's table.
The creme drop was an old-time sweet.
But God drove out the man
and placed at the east
Cherubims,
and a flaming sword which turned every way.

SONG FOR A KISS

Something quick and wet on my neck.
I whipped around, and right behind me
in the lunch line: Mary-Arkansas Greene,
grinning shy mischief
and maybe adoration.
The girl who always stared at me
during penmanship.
Anger went all over me like fire ants.
Imagining a smear of mud on my nape,
as if she had stained me with her blackness,
I reached back and tried to rub it off with my collar.
I felt like blessing her out
but didn't speak a sound.
Her grin was gone.
I rubbed my neck again, but I could tell:
the kiss was there.

Third-grade year, Mary-Arkansas
moved to Little Rock, and I never saw her again.
I sometimes thought of her kiss
when the days dragged themselves
like doomed soldiers through the Delta. Towns dying,
blacks and whites forever fighting.
Sweet Willie Wine lashed to a light pole and stoned.
Sheriff's home bombed.
A young father mobbed and kicked to death at a track meet.

One high school night, "the races"
were set to rumble in downtown McCrory.
The Bloods were coming from Little Rock,
the Klansmen from the Ozarks. *This had to be settled.*
But nothing happened. I drove dead easy
down the main drag at midnight.
Calm, deserted. The wind's nonchalance.
The quiet was violence, too.

On Friday and Saturday nights, white daughters sneaked
"behind the bank" with black sons,
and disheveled white fathers sat in their cars
with handles of whiskey, shotguns
pointed straight at Plantation Subdivision.

No peace. No peace in quiet.
And so I speak. Confess. Testify.

One morning when I was seventeen,
I heard about Mary-Arkansas. The dark, exciting news,
like dirty drugs from a syringe,
coursed through the halls of tiny McCrory High.
"Remember Mary-Arkansas Greene?!
She got shot in the head last night in Little Rock!
They say she might not make it through the day."
I wanted to drive to Little Rock,
find the hospital, find her room,
walk in slow, and touch her hand.
Lean down and kiss her.
At once I felt ashamed
for dreaming that my kiss—belated blessing—
would be worth a good goddamn.
That it could heal, heal anything: her, me, home.

But Mary-Arkansas's kiss.
Soft and urgent on my neck,
sweet opposite of rope, it never left me.
I think it never will.

EASY

This
is a bowl of rice cooked
in cinnamon milk. I'm clinking it down
in the middle of 1990.
Behold:
a giant, pink, heart-shaped cookie.
I've cut the hot milk cake, and now
I'm mixing up mimosas. I'm building an altar
to Easy Lee.

Easy
is my spirit
wife. She loves
a sporting man.
Here hangs my Michael Jordan Starter jacket.
Now I need
some music. Two unlabeled cassettes
stare out the windows
of my jam box, their spools, like eyes
of owls, stuck in senile, crotchety panic.
The batteries are low:
push play, it sounds like demons.

I uncork a bottle
of strawberry wine. I'm trying to remember
what moving from thought to thought
felt like in the year before the Web.
This is wild
marshmallow blossom, dried and crushed,
from our wedding in the woods.

I now present
the first of two aquariums
I kept as a boy. I must have been
eight or nine when my grandfolks

bought it for me. Alive
with wavy golden fish, it's confetti
in slow motion, like a happy memory
turning scary.

Vicki from *Small Wonder*
is a girl-bot
with a control panel in her back.
Her reruns play
in black and white
on this tiny television, and I'm building
an altar to Easy Lee.

I'm coloring a picture of the Mater Dolorosa
with the nubs
of my boyhood crayons. Auburn
for drawing hair,
tawny for filling in the skin
"high yellow." I'm coloring
the girl I wed
before escaping childhood. The wedding
was the men's idea. I didn't want
a ghost queen, but I got one anyway. Easy
wore a teenaged girl to marry me in. A virgin
named Gladleen.

This
is the shirt I wore for the wedding.
I'm using it
to clean the blood and rust
from my guitar strings. Every Thursday
belongs to Easy—
cakes and spells and songs. I dream
her into bed. The men said never
take another lover. Said if I did,
the love would be cursed.
The love has been cursed.
I'm stacking lovers' photographs, a luckless deck

of cards. With my very days and years, I'm building
an altar to Easy Lee.

I now present the second aquarium.
It stands for the worship party where
Easy commandeered *my* body.
It happened
in the Revel woods, off Highway 33.
I didn't remember at all. I'm not sure
where my self went off to. Doubt
I got it all back. The men called a self
a "global non." The men said I
put a dress and makeup on, and wept
my face to gleaming. This aquarium,
with its fish of many colors,
means there are
alien selves inside my head, an otherworldly
slow swirl
of notions and emotions.

Here's a photograph of the girl
named Gladleen. Once,
by chance, I glimpsed her at a basketball game.
We were still
in junior high. She sat in the stands, eating
Frito pie with a white plastic spoon and
rooting for Palestine-Wheatley. She was
a real girl I didn't know at all.

Wine all over the altar
is for the nights, the nights I walk—wine spilled
for the stranger, and the women since
my wedding. Two or three of them loved me,
never knowing I wasn't free.

Spilled wine for the dark, wet streets
bleeding red light, bleeding
red light, red light in the rain.

FOR TESS, FROM THE BLUE DOOR TAVERN, 2010

Most of my Blue Door memories are blurred,
seen through thirteen glasses darkly, but you
come through—arch grin, a stinging bourbon kiss.
Something about the sky tonight, the way
the stars excruciate, beckons me back.
I showed up every day at dusk, alone.
I had no clue why I was still alive.
Do you remember the night we met? You sauntered
over and took a seat in my dark booth.
You said the ice in my bourbon looked like crystal
foreskins. It did. I liked you right away.
You beat me at pool and beat me at beer. Told stories
about your father's Do Lord Liberation
Station: 'The Travelling Trailer-Park Revival.'
One night we cashed out, strolled down weedy sidewalks,
said poems to one another. You worried aloud
about your younger brother. I feared I loved you.
My mind typed out your words and then deleted
them so the quotation marks could 69.
That's not being a good listener. But
I wasn't up to risking hope, except
for silence, sex, a total eclipse of my face.

In case you wonder what's become of me:
all of a weird sudden, I'm city slicked
in mega-world. It's easy to confuse
Longhorn and crucifix, and hard to feel my life.
Tess, I am many bewildering years old.
Your never lover. You'd be surprised how often
I think of you, pray for your drunken brother.
How often I've remembered our one walk,
poems on our lips in the city of dead bulbs.
You were there. Louisiana power and light.
Thank you for being me a sure way home.
When I was there, I wasn't. I'm so sorry.

A MESSAGE FOR THE KING

You can't miss it. There's a plywood sign,
its white paint zebra'd
with weathering, that says BRUSH ARBOR REVIVAL.
Jalopies line the road and flap
their rusty wings. A peculiar people
wade the night, the boot-smooching mud.

Under the moon the silver rice.

King David, half-naked
on the levee, gets in a godly tizzy and speaks
in tongues. It sounds like "Come in a Honda,
leave in a Volvo. Come in a Honda, leave in a Volvo.
Econolodge: thirty-nine, ninety-nine."

The queen, unmelting, hisses
mistily from her tower, sees
his praise arms
flung up filthy white
like a gas-station toilet seat.

David waves at her window and laughs.

"Honda Honda Hyundai."

He lays hands on the people.

"God, turn these silver fillings
into heaven-highway gold.

"O God, bless this little infinite
a-growing in Mama's belly.

"Come in a Honda,
come a Honda, come a Honda.
Come in a Hon', Econo-ninety-nine-a-Honda."

Silver o'clock, and David dances Arkansas.

Work your way
into the scrum. Tell the king
we cheer him, we love him for these nights.
But before you kiss his face and go,
urge him
not to be too proud not to be too proud.

THE NIGHT I SACRIFICED 5,000 RED-WINGED BLACKBIRDS

Whenever they claim the water oak,
        shivering leaflike in its bare, cold limbs,
    and night is blackbird dreams,
           or morning comes begrudgingly home
    and their wild feathers soak up all the dark,
I remember New Year's Eve, two thousand ten.
    Welcome to Beebe, Your Dream Hometown.
    Your real hometown.

I remember twilight,
      stopping at the fireworks stand.
You were still a girl human,
      poised and posh,
          so very okay. I remember
          rum and nightfall:
    your black lashy eyes, black sheeny hair,
      sudden sex in your voice. I remember
a thousand tendril-talons pulling themselves from your roots
      and tangling out toward me as you became a wilderness.
      Till then it was only love.

    It got dark.
      Fireworks blew inside the night
and swam upstream, careful
      not to fertilize the moon. I was nothing but the burst
and the black sky it lives on: pure
      Roman candle
      aiming through you right at God.

Graveyard crosses to the north
      and railroad crosses to the south,
    I said the spell. I still remembered it. I remember
    almost midnight,
    when it started raining blackbirds. *Let the sparks go up*

and the darks come down.
　　You tackled me to the earth,
　　　　defiled my body, burned me
with firecrackers. Your talons made my skin sing red.
　　Every bit of you and me—
　　　　every cell was singing.

Morning arrived, you hated me so much: me
　　the bringer of your dark dead birds.
　　I held one in my palm: like a firework charred
silent. The birds cursed your rooftop
　　and confused your scientists.
　　All those beaks and eyes, they filled your wading pool
　　and clogged your swing-set ruts.

　　What is tonight about? Have you come
　　　for my confession? I confess:
　　　　I never loved
you or myself. Put this down:
　　　I live my spells and nothing else,
　　take my fellow animals wherever
I am most afraid to go. I know
　　　　I make for such sickening aftermath:
the dark dead facts, the bloodstains
　　memoried into your feathers forever.

REVENANT

The vision strikes at a high school football game.
During the prayer I hear somebody breathe
and grunt: a rotten girl struggling to climb
up from the netherworld below my feet.

Her tweedy face, like olive Donegal, pokes
into the space beneath the next row down.
Bawling "I love you!," she claws my ankles, rakes
them with her nails. I move away and scan

the crowd: everyone's looking. The girl yells
my name, her curses lacerate the air.
As the wordy reverend's amplified voice drawls
and drones, wherever I move, the child is there.

An old man gasps to see her hungry hands
scratching the dark, and asks me why I'd cram
a little dead girl underneath the stands.
Somehow I know: she is the one my mom

miscarried. How did she grow outside a woman
from miniature red alien to this?
She disappears inside me like a demon.
I feel her—my body is a haunted house.

PROSIMETRUM 2: BODY SHOTS

1

Several phone calls and a couple of road trips later, I found the girl they called Gladleen. All that questing, and she was down the street the entire time. She ran a restaurant in my city. We arranged a get-together, and I met her at her private studio above the restaurant. She was working on a sculpture called *The Afterlife*: two fat-ass, taxidermied mice playing Twister on a Wonder Bread bag. The artist stood to greet me. All tall and tight in her waxed black jeans. Red powder-brush hair and a fitted T-shirt that said "Support Southern Rock." She reached out her hand, I gave it a squeeze. "I like it," she said. "Nice, firm dude grip. Don't present me no bouquet of noodles. Hi, I'm Gladleen."

2

I started meeting Gladleen for drinks, mostly at her restaurant. Both of us were plowing through breakups. We were at the mercy of ourselves, a place you never want to be.

One time, she said, "Let me see a picture of your lost lady-love." I pulled one up on my phone and handed it over. She handed me her phone and made me watch a video of her ex. He was sitting on a tailgate, muttering unintelligible things to a My Buddy doll. The star of the video was Gladleen's disembodied laughter.

3

For a time we avoided discussing our odd past in Arkansas. Fear of awkwardness, I guess, but avoidance itself is awkward. One evening at the restaurant, Gladleen finally asked me why, as a boy, I had been willing to "marry a thighjacker."

I tried to explain: "I remember when I was little, when you walked into McDonald's, they had these life-sized cardboard cutouts of teenage burger flippers, but if you moved around and got a different perspective, the burger flippers would hologram into older franchise managers wearing white shirts and dark neckties and grinning themselves silly."

"Yes," Glad said. "I remember those. Your point would be?"

"Lot of times when I was maybe four or five," I said, "when I would pray to Jesus, and think about those pictures of him hanging sensually, half-naked, on the cross, with his flowy hair, lean body, and small wrists and ankles, he would start hologramming into a woman in my mind. And I would feel ecstatic but also wretchedly guilty about it. To make amends with God, I'd force myself to detonate the body of the lady Jesus in my brain, or I would cross her out with thick, dark, imaginary lines. I hated doing that terrorism so much. I can't even tell you. I wound up having to see a psychiatrist because the detonations and lines got so intense, they started happening on their own, almost constantly, till I couldn't even concentrate at school."

Glad poured me a gill of scotch neat, herself one too, and clinked me with her wonted toast: "Wonder Twin powers, activate." Then she said, "You know, the night you got married, my aunt dragged me into the swamp because she was helping with the wedding preparations. She was keeping me for a few weeks and didn't have anybody to leave me with. I had never seen any religious ceremony of any kind except at the COGIC church. I didn't know the first thing about what was happening in those woods that night. But when they started singing, the drumming noise looked like it was rippling and looping all over the air. Lassoed me something fierce." She squinted into the memory. "When I woke up, I was still a virgin, but my body wasn't."

4

After one of our many drinking nights at Gladleen's restaurant, I started staggering down the street, looking for a taxi, addled as hell. I stopped, almost lost my balance, feeling quoozy. Looked up and watched a cirrus cloud mummify the moon. Right beside me: a bar and grill with outdoor TVs blaring. I fished my phone out of my pocket and stared at it. Too drunk to realize I had picked the worst possible spot for making a call, I dialed my ex-girl.

Ashlee gets the left hand going here . . . There's another one to the midsection!

"What's up? You too drunk to hail a cab?"

North-south position now—hammers away to the side of the carcass!

"Glad? I was trying to call—"

"Oh my god! I *told* you not to drunk-dial her!"

I looked down at my phone. "What? How did you—?"

. . . boom with the right hand again! . . . End of the round! A few more seconds, she might have pounded her out!

Glad was practically shouting: "I put my number under her name in your phone!" By now I could see Glad walking toward me down the street.

Or is it over? It is over! It is over!

THE SONG—

1

Day one of the art experiment,
Glad takes my clothes off
and wields her fancy camera. Shoots me all over
at close range. The camera, like a playfully vicious dog,
snaps at me
again and again, up one side and down the other.
All the while, the artist mumbles strangeness.

"Your brother Set persuaded you
to crawl into a box."

Kneecap. Snap.

"The hand of one
baptizing in the wilderness. One for Montenegro."
Snap. "One for Mount Athos." Snap.

"One for Istanbul." Snap. "All these yearning, burning bones."

"Something to feed the catfish." Snap.

"When you refuse the maenads grabbing—"

Left foot, right foot. Snap. Snap.

At the end she says "decapitate"—
snap—
and shoots my face.

Makes me leave my blue jeans there, and gives me a pair of shorts.

2

Day two, Glad gets me drunk.
Three o'clock in the morning, restaurant long since closed,
she walks me up to her dark studio.

"Meet Eurydice," Glad says and flips the lights on.

I see my photos glued all over
a shirtless, headless, thin, originally male
mannequin. My jeans recut
to wrap the legs tight. A dark-blue football helmet
mounted on the back, suggesting a woman's ass.
Pocked orbs like cannonballs glued
to the chest, in a plain white bra.

I kneel before Eurydice. Up close,
to my hazy brain, the blue jeans' zipper
turns into Tutankhamun's death mask.

"Get off your knees," Glad says.
"Pick her up and carry her downstairs."
I do.
"All right. Now lay her down on the bar."
Glad places a lime wedge
where the headless mannequin's mouth

would be. "Undo her jeans
and lower them a little, not too much.
Now lick."
I wetten Eurydice. Glad gives me
a sea salt grinder, and I make it snow.
I lick again. She takes a bottle of Kah, pours
tequila on Eurydice's belly. I slurp it up.
Glad says, "Time for the lime
kiss. Greg, repeat after me."

I'm looking for the face . . .

I'm looking for the face I had . . .

*I'm looking for the face I had
before the world was made . . .*

I bend down slowly. Take
the lime between my teeth.

WHAT'S AWFUL

There's this simple little animal
        shivering in the tangled brush
of your pride. It wants
        to come out of hiding,
    find another to play with.

    You've no idea what to do.

You rip it out and douse it with lighter fluid.
    Set it on fire.
Bind the charred body to the train tracks.
    That about does it.

You go to the swamp one evening,
minutes before the chicken truck
    arrives to drop remains.
Night darkens, and the gators wait,
        all ominous silence and glowing eyes.

    You toss it at their suddenly snapping mouths.

When it crawls
        out of the algae some days later,
bloodied and bedraggled, and
        limps to your feet, you know it
    will never be right again.

    You almost kill the thing.

    What's awful is,
        you never can.

STRANGER, I

No one else heard
the high, discordant cymbal crash
of light when you were born,
or tastes the wild manuka
deep inside your thinking,
like the soft syllable
this.
No one else felt
the fear when you, alone
at ten years old, glimpsed a ghost
bleeding black from his mouth
and clutching a white rose.
Five years later, when the eyes and cries
of a shadowy panther
scared you from the woods.
Or later still, as you became
the ghost, the panther.

I am the only one. But I
can never know you. Not as the women
know you, the ones you peel and eat.
Or the men
whose faces you have ruined with your fists.
You need
your clingstone women,
your breakable men.
But know this: when the last hours
thin to pale shreds, seconds
that cannot warm you,
and you fall, small and astonished, into
endless white dark,
I will say your thoughts
to you. You will say my thoughts
to me. I
alone will die
with you.

PRAYER TO ISIS

The fact is is
that I live in a blur of night.
The reason is is
that I frequent Midtown Lounge, the poets' pub.
The thing is is
during the 1990s, millions of Americans
took to using the double *is*.
Our grandfolks in their gliders
thought the world had caught a stutter.

The secret
is is *is is*
launched from Midtown—some radical's
faint, quaint syntactivism, which grew
into a sex scandal.
Now, terrified of feeling
truthless, ruthless
men play holy men. The mask with a knife,
your wicked twin, tries not to hear
the wind's ecstatic moan or feel
the beautiful lust
in a belly dance of desert.

Tonight, our table mocked a kid
for mentioning inspiration.
One *poiétés* did a spoof: "It's like. The page
is my holy wife, yeah? And she gives birth
to a chubby, ugly, perfect little poem!
I look down and wonder
whether I was even involved.
Yeah?
I gawk like Joseph gawked
at the little swaddling Jesus:
'Is you is
or is you ain't my baby?'"

Our lục bát specialist,
Candy Allen Sutherby, stays angry
at the greats: Shakespeare, Dickinson, Yeats . . .
Activist poet Janet Wayne
stays angry, too. For her, for now,
it's all about eco. Earlier tonight,
she said, "The truth is is
poets ought to write about nothing
but fricking fracking
till it stops!"
"Oh, Janet," Candy said. "Using verse
the way you do is like
holding up an ancient vase
to shield your town from missiles."

Zoning out, I wandered into a memory, into
a stormy boyhood day.
The rusted yellow glider, blown over
in high winds, looked like a man facedown
in pain or prayer.

The point is is I remembered and I remember
remembering. There might just be a me.

Having cigs and swigs
with Candy, I said, "Our crew
has never gotten the hang of the
world. We don't even have our own suffering."
"You wanna suffer?" Candy asked.
"I'd rather enjoy," I said, "but I don't. Do you?"
"I enjoy Midtown."
"To me," I confessed, "it's hell deprived of its dignity."
"Dignity?"
"The dignity of agony," I said. "Sometimes I—"
"Dante was such a genius!" he blurted out.
"Everybody knows it,
no one can deny it. Let's all just jack off
to the fact that Dante was such a genius!"

From there I got destroyed on Maker's.
Candy stuffed me into his car
and pointed it toward my house.

AT THE END OF LIFE'S ROPE
REACH FOR THE HEM OF HIS ROBE?

"When do you know
postmodern indeterminacy is itself
absolute?" asked Candy. "When the advice
on a church sign ends with a question mark."

FALLING ROCK

"Falling rock?!" Candy shouted. "W. T. Fuck!
Is that a good idea?
Whose genius notion was it to build a road
in the middle of a goddamn avalanche?"

Ours.

It felt good
to imagine the cliff's face
crumbling down
upon us like bitter laughter.

After Candy dropped me off,
I looked up

at a smear of stars—

then staggered inside to be
sick alone. See that
robot-looking trash bin? It ate my
upside-down-volcano head. The lava scorched
my throat, and now—
to drop an old-time eggcorn—
I've got me a horse in my voice.

It's technically tomorrow.
Goddess, where have you gone?

Four in the morning. Quiet, dark.
My spirit-body ripped apart and littering
the land. I think this
might be me
suffering. Are you there,
sister? Sister, are you
there?

SWEET TOOTH HOMELESS

You'd been gone a bad long while.
I had stopped tipsy-texting you altogether.
Deleted the bizarre home movies—
even my favorite, the Christmas one.
Remember? You were sitting on your sea-green tailgate,
arm around a My Buddy doll.
I was "womanning the camera," as you put it.
You warned Your Buddy not to let the man in red
steal the holiday in his heart,
and made up a carol on the spot
that went, "Santa ain't nothin' but Satan misspelled."
I tried to suppress my laughter, but
there it was on tape: blooming wintersweet.

You'd been gone a bad long while.
It was closing time at the restaurant—
one of those ferociously cold nights
when the wind scrapes
your face off. I was about to lock
the front door, when a filthy man
hobbled up. I cracked the door.
"Excuse me, ma'am," he said.
"May I ask you something?"

"What?"

"I used to come here with my wife," he said.

"Okay."

"Those desserts right there. On display
 under the glass. They're real, aren't they?"

"Why?"

"What do y'all do with them?
At the end of the night."

I stared at him.
Long gray beard and hair. Big damp eyes.
He looked like he was peeping through a brush pile.

"Wait for me in the alley.
It'll be a while," I said, and shut the door.
The last one out of the restaurant, I brought
a molten lava cake and made him
take his clothes off, lie down on the frozen
asphalt, and open his mouth. "Wide," I said.
"Like a baby bird."

"You're only the second woman to see me naked
since I've been grown," he confessed.

Sickly ribcage like an old forgotten culvert.

I dropped crumbs, one by one.
Some he caught in his mouth.
Some got webbed in his beard.
He closed his eyes to savor
the flavor. "I thought we were happy," he said.
"One day she told me
my shadow was staining her
carpet." I dropped the cake and ground it
into the muddy gravel with my bright black shoe.
"Lick it up," I said, and left.

The next night, I was expecting him.
I didn't know
what I wanted. To apologize.
To pop him with my crop.
To fuck him natural.
At closing time I peered down the empty street,

swept bare by the shushing wind.
An empty white bag danced along the sidewalk
like a ghost lost and getting used to it,
merrily enough.

The homeless man with a sweet tooth
never came back for more,
while here I am, writing you
this letter. Swearing
it's the last.

WELCOME TO THE OLD CATHEDRAL

My name is Madison—I'll be your server tonight.

I don't know where I am.
Where am I?

You're at the—

I'm at a tony restaurant off the square.
Crazy rain trying to bring the stained glass
to life. But—

How silly of me. Of course you know where you are.

I know about the restaurant and the rain.
Very urgent rain.
But where am I?

You are here.

I want to be there.
I'm more of a diner kind of a diner.
When I was young, I frequented a diner
on a movie set. The director had disappeared,
and the actors had forgot it wasn't real.
I've wondered if I wasn't one of them.
The owner, Bill, had a weird dog
that looked like Benjamin Franklin.
Bill and the dog would come and greet me.
"Fish and chips and a cherry Sprite," I'd say.

"Faith will be your waitress," Bill would tell me.
"She'll swing over in a minute to take your order."

I am Madison. I'll be taking care of you tonight.

And there was a baby, a diminutive *flâneur,*
wobble-walking all about the set, making a voice noise
like a straw fucking a milkshake lid.

I am Madison. I'll be taking care of you tonight.

Is it true what they say, Madison,
that Michael McDonald and Garth Brooks
are playing a secret concert just a few doors down
and Elvis will split the eastern sky at sunrise?

For our soup du jour,
we have our invisible butterfly soul.
That's gonna come with seven Australian Painted Lady souls
dissolved in hot holy water
tinged with a suspicion of jasmine.

It's not that McDonald has gone country, you see.
Rather, Garth is doing blue-eyed soul.
They're treating the audience to some universal evergreens
like "Let's Stay Together" and "Burning Both Ends of the Night."

For our special—

Shhh. If you close your eyes,
you can hear "What a Fool Believes."
Michael McDonald singing through his beard.

For our special we have our steamed heart of hummingbird.
That's gonna be served with a complex reduction
of unrequited Gemütlichkeit and transubstantiated red wine.

Mad, you aren't listening.
Let's go seeing.
Let's go being.
Roads agush with rivery rain. Lady legs ascamper
on the square. Frogs hopping

like tiny sparks of apocalypse. Garth Brooks.
It's all happening.

Can I start you off with the thirtieth stanza
of Keats's "The Eve of St. Agnes" whispered
by Li-Young Lee into a hardy flapjack scroll?

You're right: nothing's happening.

Can I go home?

You may go wherever you like.

But do I want to go home
to the elevator's déjà vu,
the mirror's dyslexia?

You may go whenever you like.

But where? Will I want to go home
if the King comes back and no one notices
and the water won't turn to blood
and the dead are busy
getting their pH tested
by the county extension agent?

You may go wherever you like.

If I do go home, what then?

Hummingbird heart.

Tell me, Mad. If I go home,
will I sit there and smile stupidly
like a Charlie Chaplin doll
years after the ventriloquist has shelved him?
Locked out of the cathedral

and decades from my diner,
I'll be a non sequitur without the Pringles.

You may go whenever, wherever you like.

Where did the shamans go,
the strange men with their drums and dreams?

I'll be taking care of you tonight.

I miss that gal who took care of me at the diner.
I miss her bathtub drain-stopper necklace:
silver beads, white plastic pendant.
One time, when "Fields of Gold" was playing,
she looked up at the speakers
and said, "O Sting, where is thy death?"
I loved her low voice and worshipped the golden calf
above each of her roller skates.
I miss old Bill and Benjamin Franklin. I miss
the wobbling baby. But the set
has vanished into desert.

Just as noun verb, so too does other noun.

I don't understand.

Faith will be your waitress.

FOLLY

And God saw every thing that he had made . . .
   —from Genesis

The author of two books at twenty-nine,
Abraham gave a talk near Charleston when
I lived in her swank slums, lost but okay
with being not okay. We lounged at the beach
till dusk. He marked exams while folks around us
gathered their things in the last cast of sun
and coaxed their sandy-leggèd kids away.
"The only texts read by these fools I teach
are their illiterate comrades' messages,"
intoned Professor Abe. "Listen to this:

Grandma knows best, as Flannel O'Donnell states
in 'A Hard Man Is Good to Find.' . . . Yeats
goes crazy with 'The Second C-U-M-
M-I-N-G.' . . . The poet Thomas Gray
eludes to pain in his short story known
as 'Allergy in a Country Churchyard.'" "That's
brilliant," I said. "It's going in a poem."
"Just a bad sentence. Don't get carried away."
"Bad, brilliant—sometimes it's a blurry line.
You don't know what you're doing till it's done."

"Poets play," Abe explained. "A scholar has
to mind the basics"—voltage in his voice
from hours of bickering. Gone quiet, I
revisited a childhood memory verse . . .
"earthquakes in divers places" . . . The man who taught
me Sunday school said, "Think about it, boys
and girls: they had three earthquakes last July
in California. Rest assured, there's divers
bailing off bridges, cliffs, and God knows what
out there, like stars a-shooting through the daylight."

Which sparked another memory, of the college
class in which Abe and I had met: To engage
our groggy brains, the young instructor rose,
armed with his NIV, and all but sang
a passage. Next to me, a wizened preacher
cracked her King James and squinted at the page.
"What all does David carry when he goes
to fight Goliath?" we were asked. "A sling,"
Abe answered, "and some rocks, five for good measure."
"And scrip," the preacher added. "That's short for scripture."

The teacher praised her vision and insisted
she tell us all about it. "Not to intrude,"
intruded Abe, "but let me help the reverend.
Scrip is the King James word for pouch or satchel."
I said inside, as an unbroken wave
reared up—white messy mane, audacious head:
Meaning Control's chief officers pretend
they don't pretend. Their world is right. It's factual.
But as for me and my heart, we will love
our faults and legends, and let those divers dive.

Reading the vellum sky, Abe said, "I hoped
you'd scored an adult role by now and dropped
this poet pose." He stood, folded his chair.
"It's getting sad." The Director Of The Cosmos
had spoken—*end your private play, cut cut*—
because I wouldn't work within a script
bound at the top with concertina wire
and do my sentence. "No funds," he said, "no house,
no rules. An artiste! Sent here to write and not
be written." He turned to go. "Good luck with that."

As night sank in, one boy came back to dance
the shore, all flapping hair and flitting hands:
serifs upon the sky. One mako leapt
and curled midair apostrophe-like. Why had

I quietly watched my (fee fie) foe escape
as if a sheep drifting across a fence?
O magic school, reclaim the gaff he stripped
of whimsical meaning. My inner harpist vowed:
Give me five iambs, good and hard, I'll drop
that philistine with basics from the scrip.

PROSIMETRUM 3: THE HOMEMADE FIREWORKS

for Alex Taylor

THE STORY—

1

The hitman my Aunt Laverta hired to kill her blind husband, Bill, turned out to be an undercover cop. She did five years in the Pine Bluff penitentiary.

An excerpt from a letter she wrote my Aunt Charlene from prison:

> I Can remember When I was three years Old, Dad Carried me on his back acrost a field to Church every Sunday, and he Would Walk about two Miles of a Morning with us when we went to school and the Sloughs would be up, and full of Water, he Carried us one at a time on his back. And Daddy Would Come through the rain, sleet, snow or What ever and bring us hot Kentucky-Wonder Brown-bean's and some of the best Corn bread I ever ate, at lunch time, he always made the best corn-bread, I can Still see him coming acrost that scope of woods wearing a brown leather cap, the ear Muffs down on his ears, and a pr. of kaki pants on, And I Can still remember the Other Children who was not that fortunate as to have some-one bring a hot lunch to them, Some had no lunch at all, poor Mom and dad always provided for us as best they could, We all worked and shared what we had, We were a clost happy family.

2

One time my Uncle Leon and I were picking sugarhaws for Christmas jelly, and I said, "I had this student from Memphis last semester in my freshman comp class. His name was Sylvester Peoples. Nice kid, personality plus. But he never could learn my last name. On his final essay, he put my name down as 'B. R. Wondervillage.'"

Uncle Leon laughed. He said, "My preacher calls me Brother Derville Brown. Lot of folks have trouble with our name." He stripped a twig of its haws. As they were pinging in his pan, he asked me, "Did you set Sylvester straight?"

"I showed him what he had written," I said, "and told him it made my year. I asked if he was issuing a challenge to my whole life: *Be our wondervillage.*"

3

My late grandfather Herbert Edward Brownderville. Shards of biography.

Uncle Leon: "Daddy had them big old stovepipe arms. He would saw a tree down with a crosscut saw *by himself,* and then saw it up in lengths, and then he'd take a broadax and hew that thing out square, which is no easy task, and make it slick, too. He was so good with a broadax, he could do it—that's an art. And then he'd pick that dude up and carry him out of the woods on his shoulder."

Alton Ray Brownderville (my father): "Daddy was forty-five years old when I was born. He'd already had his teeth pulled by then, and didn't have the money for false teeth, so I never knew him with teeth. But he could eat meat and everything. He'd just gnaw a piece of meat off and gum it and swallow it down."

Uncle Leon: "For three years when I was a little-bitty kid, me and Daddy and Mama lived in a tent. Daddy packed kerosene and ashes down as our floor—shiny gray like cement. I think the kerosene kept bugs away."

Aunt Alta Mae (my father's twin sister): "One evening, when it was getting to be dusky dark, Mama and Daddy and several of us kids was walking home from the cotton field, and it started hailing real bad. I saw one hailstone as big as a trailer hitch. We all sheltered in a thick fencerow and waited for it to pass. When we come out, the air was full of white feathers and there was dead geese everywhere, scattered all over our forty. Daddy gathered up some in his pick sack for us to cook."

Alton: "Dad and Cecil Hubbard never got along too well. Their properties joined on the east side of Mama and Daddy's forty, and there was a fence between the two properties. And this horse of ours named Buck had his head between the barbed wire eating grass. Since he was eating on Hubbard's side of the fence, why, he just opened fire on him. Looked like buckshot to me. So the horse, out of panic, ran at a full gait back up towards the house and jumped the fence that separated our backyard from our pasture, and run into the front yard where Daddy was. And the blood was just shooting out—I don't know—fifteen or twenty feet, it looked like, every time his heart would beat. It was pitiful. And he had so many holes in him that there was no way to save the horse, but Daddy couldn't shoot him. Just couldn't pull the trigger. You get attached to animals, especially when you make a living with them and depend on them. And looked like the old horse's eyes was, you know, 'Do something to help me.' And there was nothing to do. It's funny how animals have a—I think they have a sense that they're hurt really bad. Daddy got Bob Houston, Laverta's first husband, to come over and put him down."

Uncle John: "One morning I climbed away up high in the toothache tree, and I looked down and seen Daddy arranging and rearranging a stack of firewood to make it look just so. I never could figure out what he was up to."

Aunt Charlene: "Daddy could strictly play down the glory. He rigged him up a homemade brace that set down over his shoulders and held the French harp up to his lips. That way, he kept his hands free so he could pick his guitar."

Alton: "Daddy couldn't afford good, thick socks or insulated boots, so on a cold fall night, he'd wrap his feet up in newspaper and put his knee boots on and go out scrapping, stripping bolls. Regularly cotton would bring thirty cents a pound, but after it was picked once and you were stripping bolls, you'd only get about ten cents a pound. It was a lot of work for a little of nothing, but he'd be out there with a pick sack late at night when water was standing in the rows and frozen to a solid sheet of ice."

Uncle John: "I've seen Daddy laying in the bed holding his twelve-gauge, long-tongue shotgun up and down his chest with the barrel under his chin and the hammer back. I've seen him pour a quart of gasoline in a jar and drink it down. Mama made him swallow raw eggs, so he would throw up. But the worst memory of all was one afternoon, along about dusk, when the whole family was out in the yard, and Mama and Daddy had a round. Daddy took his twelve-gauge and walked along the levee clean over to the other side of the rice field, out of sight, and fired the gun. Evidently he just shot it into the air, but we didn't know that. I reckon he was trying to shock Mama or God or somebody into showing him some pity. But there we were, just little kids, running around, panicking: 'Daddy's dead! Daddy's done gone and shot his self!'"

4

An excerpt from a prison letter from Aunt Laverta to Aunt Charlene—

Dad used to cut us a limb off of Our Big Old Cedar tree over in the back field for a Xmas tree. I can still amagin that I can smell the cedar scent at Xmas time, It Was the Only Kind we had, And you know a person always thinks of home at Xmas time.

They sure did put all the Magic in Xmas for us kids, Dad would take Red hot Coals of fire out of the Old Box heater, lay them on the chop block & he would draw back & hit them with the side of the ax or with a sledge hammer, the sparks at night Were so pretty, then all of a sudden Mom would come out & join in the fun, And then not long afterwards while we were still watching the fireworks, we would hear a stick of wood hit the side of the house or some sorta noise, any way we knew that had to be Old Santa Clause, then we would run into the house fast as we could go to see what Old Santa had left for us, Most of the time I'd get a doll & set of dishes, but one year when you was a baby, the bowl-weavels got the cotton, and all we got was a pr. jersie gloves to pull the nottie bowls of cotton with, we felt

so let down & sad, but that was Only one, we had a lot of good
ones, those were good days, Well, I just looked out the window
& Its snowing now, so that Completes the story I just told you
and it is all a true story. Guess I'll close for now Sis, have a Very
Merry Xmas & May God Bless all of you, By far my worst Xmas
ever. Your Sister.

THE SONG—

"Word I was in my life alone,
Word I had no one left . . ."

—from "Bereft," by Robert Frost

Kentucky fictioneer, my friend, old friend,
do you remember texting me
from Walmart last December?
"Out Christmas shopping," you wrote,
"I have come to the conclusion that this country is
done for."
I texted, "What do you see?"
"General malaise," you answered.
"Gawking droolers jean clad and florid.
Gaudy, fat wives
and aghast husbands clutching
scented candles.
Done for."

As I received these magical tidings,
I was in the house
alone, per usual. I was standing before a mirror,
my face all santa-claused
with shaving cream. Razor to my neck.
How, I asked myself, *does one
come through the Holidays?*

It takes a wondervillage. Which,
Sylvester Peoples notwithstanding, I am not.

The Christmas onslaught comes
again, and here we are, bud, one year closer
to our funerals, eschewing candlehood
and yet a little envious. You ask me,
"Does our work amount to anything?
What would our grandfathers think?"
You say you're putting down your pen for good.

I'm in the house alone. The night
is quiet, and I can't fight off your questions.
I'm thinking about mysterious old Herbert Edward.
He was a man. It's hard
for me to strip him back to that.
Not merely a son, father, husband, grandfather.
A man.
An artist, too. A wizard
with a French harp and a sculptor with a broadax.
He knew nothing of Georges Braque
or *Violin and Candlestick,* but Uncle John says
from high in the toothache tree, you could catch him doing
some beautiful country cubism, working that rick of wood.

Last time I travelled home, I traipsed out to the swamp—
stopped and wondered
at a cypress trimmed
with colorful bobbers and shiny spinners and lures.
I hung my share of bobbers in that tree.
Me and Herbert Edward used to fish there,
different sloughs. I can still see him
coming across that scope of woods
with a shimmering string of bream.

I used to go out there in winter as a boy
to love the quiet. To sit by the water
and warm my hands in a dog's fur.
To see the accidental Christmas tree.
With only my dad between

me and Herbert Edward, I've had, most days,
an obscenely easy life.

I wrap my feet in newspaper
never, put my boots on, go out in the freezing rain
to scrap cotton when the middles are solid ice,
and come back late, icicles hanging off my snap-bill leather cap
never. I stack ties on a trailer not
and sit up top with my little boy,
knowing neither he nor I can swim—
the water so deep, the mules
will have to get up on their hind legs and lunge
to ford the bayou
never.

If ever my nonexistent family should have to make
a bumpy winter trip by ghost horse and ghost buggy,
I will do like Herbert Edward: heat rocks
in the old box heater, wrap them
in gunnysacks, and set them
in the floorboard. That way, my playlike wife and kids
can warm their playlike feet.

The other night, my girlfriend and I drove out of town
to see her ninety-year-old aunt.
Blood-slush cold outside. Icy raindrops,
all that bling on the trees. Luckily, my car
has heat, even heated seats. The roads were slick silver,
but we made it. Once there, my girlfriend
mostly played with the pets. The aunt and I talked
for over an hour, and she was, in a word,
unimpressed. She told my girlfriend later,
"That so-called man of yours
sat right there in my living room and *watched*
the fire go out." She paused—
let the outrage sink in. "And when we shook good-bye,"
she summed me up, "his hands were soft as snow."

I'm a walking white Christmas,
here in my obscenely easy life. But friend, old friend,
Kentucky fictioneer, the words you write
about your hurting hills
bring me closer
to Herbert Edward. They remind me what it takes, what
wrenching sacrifice, to keep
the new years coming
with their facile firework shows. You help me,
when I see those red sprays of light,
to remember Buck's blood,
and in each pop like distant gunfire,
to hear a proud man saying please.

Herbert Edward asked your questions. I could read them
in his sad squint. He probably felt like a failure
when he scooped those red-hot coals of fire,
placed them on the chopping block, and pounded
the holy Christmas out of them.
The pitifulness.

Every day, we draw back
and strike again to spark the dark.
Unbearable anticlimax. Words
return unto us
void. The child for whom we write
grows old and sins
and spends Christmas away from home, in a cold place
with kerosene and ashes underfoot.
Animals have a—I think they have a sense
that they're hurt really bad.
But maybe
in that tent, that Pine Bluff penitentiary,
when snow comes fluttering down like feathers,
the child remembers.
Let him taste Kentucky Wonder,
smell fresh cedar on your ax.

CPSIA information can be obtained at www.ICGtesting.com
Printed in the USA
LVOW11s1027041016

507213LV00003BB/356/P

9 780807 163542